Previous book by author:

Sugar and Salt: My Life with Bipolar Disorder

The Rookie's Guide to
TO BIPOLAR DISORDER

by

Jane Thompson

authorHOUSE®

AuthorHouse™
1663 Liberty Drive, Suite 200
Bloomington, IN 47403
www.authorhouse.com
Phone: 1-800-839-8640

First published by AuthorHouse   5/28/2008

ISBN: 978-1-4343-7965-8 (sc)

Printed in the United States of America
Bloomington, Indiana

This book is printed on acid-free paper.

Dedicated to:
Bruce Belland

ACKNOWLEDGEMENTS

I need to thank my doctors. Without them, I would not have the quality of life I have now, and there is a good chance I would not be alive at all. Dr. Gary Kula diagnosed me and got me over the hard part of realizing and accepting the fact that I had a mental illness. Dr. James Shupe truly listened and understood. Dr. Rudy Molina worked with me through crises. Dr. Stephen Crane helped me through changes in my life. My current psychiatrist, Dr. Kerry Halfant, keeps me stable and encourages my writing.

Meg Frank encouraged me to write this book, as did Clayton O'Claerach, who also offered help and useful suggestions. Kira Cox read it in its infant stages and gave me suggestions. Mary Jo Casey helped with the concept and with the execution of the book, and read and reread it until she was sure it was right.

I also want to thank the readers of my previous book, **Sugar and Salt: My Life with Bipolar Disorder**, who have encouraged me to continue writing.

The publishers, Authorhouse, have made it easy to get my words into print.

And, of course, Bruce Belland, lead singer of the Four Preps, who has always been in my corner and who has contributed the wonderful Foreward to this book.

Jane Thompson
Georgetown, Texas
jtokc@yahoo.com

FOREWARD

We all have heroes we admire and look up to.

Jane Thompson is one of mine. Not just because of what she has become but because of what she has *overcome.*

Her willingness to share her ordeal and her long and painful triumph over it in order to help others, puts Jane in a brave and selfless category that goes beyond heroism to the purest form of altruism.

The book you hold in your hand is a gift from someone who simply refused to let her bipolar diagnosis define or limit her life. And it can help you do the same.

Jane has done the research, braved the setbacks and bumps on her long and challenging road to recovery so that you might benefit from the hard lessons she has learned.

She has walked the walk – and now she talks the talk. In plain, direct, easy to understand language. And what she has to say can make a powerful difference in your life.

The medal she wears for her heroism will be the smiles on the faces of the thousands that will be helped by this brave book.

I am proud to call Jane Thompson my friend.

Bruce Belland
Woodland Hills, CA.

INTRODUCTION

I wrote this book to introduce those who have been recently diagnosed with bipolar disorder to some basic concepts about the disorder. There is a huge amount of information to be taken in when diagnosed with this illness; I tried to make it short and easily understood. I also wanted to offer some resources in the form of books, support groups, and message boards to the person who does not know where to turn.

The most important thing I want to get across is the fundamental necessity of getting treatment and sticking with it to attain stability and prevent episodes from reoccurring. Thanks to my doctors, a good teaching hospital, and my own persistence, I have been stable on medications for 20 years. Watching others struggle gives me the feeling that I am obligated to help them as much as possible to reach that goal.

I apologize if I have left out your favorite Website, support group, book, or message board.

AND SO IT BEGINS

When I hung up the phone, I knew it was over.   And I had sworn this was the last one.

Actually, this one sneaked in under the radar.   I had always had problems with relationships and had given up on having a successful one.   This guy spent six weeks wining and dining me, sending me flowers and convincing me with his sensitivity that he was the one I could trust.   I played, no hell, I didn't play, I was hard to get until after weeks of testing him, I realized that if I got breast cancer, this dude wouldn't run out on me.   He knew my big secret, and that hadn't scared him.   He loved my cats, missed me when I was out of town, and had seen me and didn't flinch right after I woke up.   He thought I looked great just as I was and insisted I was a talented writer.   A real keeper.   His name was Mark.   He'd come over in the middle of the week, then take me out for breakfast in the morning just because he couldn't wait until the weekend to see me.   The cat would sleep on his shirt and get cat hair all over it, and he would just laugh.   On top of all his other good features, he was good-looking..   He was funny and wanted to know all about me.

Just after I made the decision that I was in love with him, he didn't show up for a Saturday date and I didn't hear from him all weekend.   Now that set off some alarm bells; when I did not hear from him on Monday, I just had to know what was going on.   So I called him up.   "What happened?" was all I said (by this time he recognized my voice on the telephone without any other identification).   After all, you do have to assume that something big at work or home came up; but then, of course, you still wonder why you didn't get a phone call.   His answer? A simple one: "I'm seeing someone else." I just hung up the phone.   I knew all I needed to know.   I was flabbergasted.   I couldn't even figure out how he had time to even think of someone else -- I hadn't had a clue.   And now, so suddenly, he was finished with me.   After getting so close to me, convincing me that he really cared about me, he was done.   And I had just started.

I was blind with fury and regret.   Did he really think that he could stop paying attention to me with no consequences? Did he think that he could just forget me? That I would go away quietly? How could he just dump me with no regard to my feelings or my future? Well, he couldn't.   All I could think about was how I felt and how I wanted him to pay attention to me. I wanted to be the most important thing in his life.   My mind was blank except for that one thought.   The feelings were overwhelming; the urge to do something to relieve those feelings was overpowering.

The only thing is, that didn't happen.   The suicide, I mean.   The rest happened. I'm bipolar, or manic-depressive, but I'm stable on medication. After I hung up the phone, I felt a lot of the same things I described. And I cried. And I wrote a poem.   That's all.

From **Sugar and Salt: My Life with Bipolar Disorder**

by Jane Thompson

DIAGNOSIS
DEPRESSION, BIPOLAR DISORDER, MANIC-DEPRESSION?

Even the most routine tasks of life seemed impossible, every problem seemed insurmountable....I left work every day and cried all the way home, weeping into the evening.... I blew up at the slightest thing, and work was becoming impossible. ...Every day that passed, I became more depressed. And, obsessed. I don't know how my friends put up with me during this period. ...In fact, I became isolated.

From **Sugar and Salt : My Life with Bipolar Disorder**
by Jane Thompson

You have heard about bipolar disorder, and you have a vague notion of what it is. I hope you haven't got all your information from news stories about crimes committed by those with bipolar disorder. Few people with bipolar disorder commit crimes, but of course those who do are those who get the attention. Most people with bipolar disorder live quiet lives--sometimes quiet lives of desperation. It doesn't have to be that way, but it is a hard disease to get a handle on, and most people with the disorder are not diagnosed.

You may think that you have it, or that a loved one does, but you may not know how to pin it down. Here are the signs and symptoms of the disorder:

Signs and symptoms of mania (or a manic episode) include:

Increased energy, activity, and restlessness

Excessively "high," overly good, euphoric mood

Extreme irritability

Racing thoughts and talking very fast, jumping from one idea to another

Distractibility, can't concentrate well

Little sleep needed

Unrealistic beliefs in one's abilities and powers

Poor judgment

Spending sprees

A lasting period of behavior that is different from usual

Increased sexual drive

Abuse of drugs, particularly cocaine, alcohol, and sleeping medications

Provocative, intrusive, or aggressive behavior

Denial that anything is wrong

From http://www.nimh.nih.gov/health/publications/bipolar-disorder/symptoms.shtml

Signs and symptoms of depression (or a depressive episode) include:

Lasting sad, anxious, or empty mood

Feelings of hopelessness or pessimism

Feelings of guilt, worthlessness, or helplessness

Loss of interest or pleasure in activities once enjoyed, including sex

Decreased energy, a feeling of fatigue or of being "slowed down"

Difficulty concentrating, remembering, making decisions

Restlessness or irritability

Sleeping too much, or can't sleep

Change in appetite and/or unintended weight loss or gain

Chronic pain or other persistent bodily symptoms that are not caused by physical illness or injury

Thoughts of death or suicide, or suicide attempts

A depressive episode is diagnosed if five or more of these symptoms last most of the day, nearly every day, for a period of two weeks or longer.

The experience of being fired from the best job I ever had broke my spirit. That's when I realized that I would have to apply for Social Security Disability. In the past, I had believed that was giving up, that you had to keep trying. But now I knew I had reached the point where trying wasn't going to get me there any more, that I had to admit that I was finally too ill to work.

From **Sugar and Salt : My Life with Bipolar Disorder**
by Jane Thompson

A mild to moderate level of mania is called *hypomania*. Hypomania may feel good to the person who experiences it and may even be associated with good functioning and enhanced productivity. Thus, even when family and friends learn to recognize the mood swings as possible bipolar disorder, the person may deny that anything is wrong. Without proper treatment, however, hypomania can become severe mania in some people or can switch into depression.

Sometimes, severe episodes of mania or depression include symptoms of *psychosis* (or psychotic symptoms). Common psychotic symptoms are hallucinations (hearing, seeing, or otherwise sensing the presence of things not actually there) and delusions (false, strongly held beliefs not influenced by logical reasoning or explained by a person's usual cultural concepts). Psychotic symptoms in bipolar disorder tend to reflect the extreme mood state at the time. For example, delusions of grandiosity, such as believing one is the President or has special powers or wealth, may occur during mania; delusions of guilt or worthlessness, such as believing that one is ruined and penniless or has committed some terrible crime, may appear during depression. People with bipolar disorder who have these symptoms are sometimes incorrectly diagnosed as having schizophrenia, another severe mental illness.

It may be helpful to think of the various mood states in bipolar disorder as a spectrum or continuous range. At one end is severe depression, above which is moderate depression and then mild low mood, which many people call "the blues" when it is short-lived but is termed *dysthymia* when it is chronic. Then there is normal or balanced mood, above which comes hypomania (mild to moderate mania), and then severe mania.

Another psychotic symptom is *paranoia,* in which the person believes that he or she is being watched or listened to or tracked by others. You cannot talk a person out of this symptom, it is not rational and the person does not respond to rational arguments.

If these signs and symptoms sound familiar, you will want to see a psychiatrist for a diagnosis. A general practitioner is not really qualified to make the diagnosis of bipolar disorder, because the diagnosis is not made through blood tests or scans. It is simply made through the experience of the doctor. He or she knows, by the self-reporting of the patient and through observation, whether or not the person meets the criteria for bipolar disorder. This is one reason some people have difficulty in accepting this diagnosis. The doctor can't show them anything concrete that demonstrates that they have the illness.

What if you cannot afford to just go to a psychiatrist? Many people with bipolar disorder can't work, or have been fired from a job when they realize that they need help. The disorder causes people to act out at work, stressing out and expressing themselves by saying or doing things they wouldn't do if they were healthy. I lost many jobs when I was undiagnosed; I usually worked hard and was good about showing up and being on time, but I would lose it over the small stuff or my deadlines would stress me out. Usually the bosses would "lay me off" rather than fire me, but everyone knew that I was being fired for not getting along with the other employees or for "being difficult." I tried so hard, but I could not always rise above the illness and be the perfect employee I wanted to be, and I couldn't understand why I could not. I wanted to keep my jobs more than anything, but it did not work that way. I lost social work jobs, teaching jobs, paralegal jobs, and writing jobs. At least I was consistent.

Or, if you are in the depressive phase, you may not be able to even get out of bed to get organized enough to get a job. Most people don't understand this, and they are certainly not sympathetic. They expect you to "snap out of it" and just get up and get going. They don't realize that you are incapable of working in your present mood.

This leaves you with no income to see a doctor. This may make you feel that you are in an impossible situation, but the government has set up Mental Health Clinics in the every state which see anyone with a mental illness despite their lack of income. However, it takes some persistence and patience to be seen. You have to set up an appointment for intake, then be evaluated and diagnosed, then, finally, you begin to receive treatment.

When I finally realized that there was something seriously wrong with me and that it was something that needed to be fixed, I really didn't think about it. I just picked up the phone book and looked up the Mental Health Clinic. I was in a small town in Oklahoma and didn't even know anyone. I did not ponder whether I had a mental illness; I just automatically did what I needed to do. I had absolutely no income and had no idea what could be done. I had to wait three weeks for an interview; but when I got one, I was treated well and given the help I needed. The doctor recognized right away that I was severely depressed; he later changed the diagnosis to bipolar disorder. This often happens because the patient presents in the depressed phase and after treatment, mania will flare up.

I was never charged for the medication, psychotherapy, or the counseling I received. It was all given to me freely and with the idea that once I was back on my feet I would be a contributing member of society again, and that is how it worked out, eventually. It was a long road to my successful medication and ability to work, but just the correct diagnosis gave me hope.

Some people are confused by the diagnosis, and are not ready to accept it. They can't believe that they have an illness that can't be measured scientifically, and wish to deny it. Others become angry at the suggestion that they have a mental illness and want to fight against the illness and the treatment. They balk at taking medications that they know they will have to take for the rest of their lives.

For me, the diagnosis was a relief. I now knew why I felt and acted the way I did and I was ready to move on to the treatment phase. For me it answered questions about why I had been so different all my life, why I had so many lapses of judgment and had done such stupid things that I couldn't even explain later, and why I became so depressed periodically, even becoming suicidal. I know I was surprised to learn that others are not suicidal; I thought it was just part of life to want to kill oneself. The knowledge that I had a disorder that could help to explain all these things was a big relief to me and made me want to fix my life.

BIPOLAR I AND II

We had never heard of manic-depression or bipolar disorder, but we knew our father had problems. We didn't know the diagnosis, or even that what he had was considered a mental illness. My mother handled it in such a matter-of-fact way that all of us simply lived our lives around how my father was; we just adjusted our lives to fit his.

From **Sugar and Salt : My Life with Bipolar Disorder**
by Jane Thompson

One of the things that people find most confusing is the classification of bipolar disorder into Bipolar I and Bipolar II. The fact of the matter is that it makes no difference, really, they are both the same animal. Bipolar I simply refers to a bipolar disorder that leans more to the manic side, with the person having more manic episodes and often having hallucinations and psychotic features than a person with Bipolar II. A person with Bipolar II will have more depressive episodes and he or she may not ever have true mania, but experience only *hypomania*. Neither one is more severe than the other; they just differ.

Actually, the disorder is quite individual. Even though you can meet a person with bipolar disorder and immediately feel a kinship and know that you have many things in common, it is also true that no two people experience the illness in exactly same way. I have no desire to overspend

10

in an obsessive way. When manic, I might buy something I don't need, or buy four lipsticks rather than one, but I will not put myself into debt as so many others do with the disorder. There is no explanation as to why I do not have this common symptom. If I did have it, I would not be able to resist it. It is not a case of will power, but a symptom of an illness that I would not be able to control. It becomes an obsession, a necessity, a compulsion that can't be denied.

People also differ in how often they cycle. Some people are *rapid cyclers* and may go from depression to mania in only a few weeks or months; others may go years between episodes. No one can predict which kind of person you are or your loved on is. You have to take medicine between episodes no matter how long the cycles are spaced apart to protect yourself from a debilitating depression or a mania that could destroy you life. While manias can feel good, particularly at first, they can also turn into irritable, angry outbursts that can cause you to lose your job or can ruin a relationship and they can cause monumental lapses in judgment. That, coupled with the urge to spend, can cost you your credit and your savings, plus plunge you into debt for life.

There are no special laws that deal with bipolar disorder; you don't get a "get out of debt free" card because you are bipolar. In fact you can end up in the justice system because of things done while manic or depressed. To find out more about that, read Pete Earley's book **Crazy** in which he describes what happens to the mentally ill while incarcerated.

Another consequence of bipolar disorder is suicide. The suicide rate among those with bipolar disorder is around twenty percent. You always must be aware of this and of your vulnerability. You have to remember that your depression is not forever and reach out for help when it seems that it is going to last forever.

I didn't attempt suicide, but was suicidal all during the time I was on a certain drug. I was unable to read or listen to music or to sleep. I had spent most of the time I was on this drug pacing and waiting for time to pass....

From **Sugar and Salt : My Life with Bipolar Disorder**

by Jane Thompson

OTHER TYPES OF BIPOLAR

Denial: The old "pull yourself up by your boot-straps" mentality.

...in our family, people were just the way they were. There was no suspicion of mental illness. People might be a little odd, or somewhat eccentric, but that was just their personalities. I had one cousin who suffered from severe depression. She was unable to care for herself and for her children, and her mother-in-law, my aunt, let everyone know how much she considered the woman to be weak and her son to have made a mistake by marrying her. The cousin had to be hospitalized, and that just didn't happen in good families. My cousin, according to the consensus of the family, should have been able to handle her problems without the help of mental health professionals.

From **Sugar and Salt : My Life with Bipolar Disorder**
by Jane Thompson

Besides Bipolar I and II, there is *cyclothemia*, a milder form of bipolar, in which the person suffers short periods of mild depression alternating with short periods of hypomania. It is only mild when compared with other kinds of bipolar, because it can still really disrupt a person's life. Another kind of bipolar is Bipolar NOS (Not Otherwise Specified), which is a bipolar disorder that does not fall into any of these categories.

It could be, for example, a person who suffers only hypomania and mania, with no depression.

Bipolar disorder can come in many different types. The classic bipolar disorder comes with an episode of mania which presents for several weeks or months, then slides into depression. After a few weeks or months of depression, the person returns to "normal" and may remain that way for as long as two or three years without another episode. It may be difficult to convince a person who has classic bipolar to stay on medication during the periods of dormancy, but that is the only way to prevent a life-altering episode. It often takes two episodes or more to diagnose and treat this type of bipolar disorder.

There is also rapid-cycling bipolar disorder, in which the person has four or more episodes a year. I was a rapid-cycler, and this type of bipolar keeps your life constantly upset. It may be easier to diagnose, but the person is manic so often it is difficult to get them to a doctor. I was 37 before I consulted a psychiatrist for my symptoms. Many others just live with the ups and downs, assuming that they are normal.

Another type of bipolar is post-partum, which shows itself only after the birth of a child. This can be dangerous, particularly if it goes into post-partum psychosis. It is often misdiagnosed as post-partum depression and only later determined to be bipolar disorder.

Mixed cycles can occur. In this case, the person experiences both depression and mania at the same time. This is particularly difficult to deal with, and is hard for the person to describe to the doctor and to live with. It can be managed, but only after a good diagnosis.

The only management for all these types and manifestations of bipolar disorder is medication, taken daily from the time of diagnosis. This can be difficult for people to accept, particularly when they feel fine. Medication allows for stability, and protects from the cycles that range from mania to depression and will recur if the person does not take medication.

Caution: A common reaction to any bipolar disorder (a.k.a. manic-depression), by both the person who has the disorder and/or that person's friends and relatives, is denial. "This simply doesn't happen in our family." "This can't be my friend; he/she is just moody." "Maybe he/she is just depressed; she'll pull out of it."

Bipolar disorder, or manic-depression illness, is known to be inherited. It affects between 0.5 and 1.6 percent of the total population.

From **Diagnostic and Statistical Manual of Mental Disorders**.
American Psychiatric Association (1994)

Children of persons with bipolar disorder have an increased risk of developing the disease. This risk is several times that of the general population; children of persons with bipolar disorder have a one in four chance of developing some kind of mood disorder, and a one in ten chance of developing bipolar disorder.

From **Bipolar Disorder: A Guide for Patients and Families**
by Francis Mark Mondimore, M.D.

What this means in a practical sense is that if the genes for bipolar disorder are present in your family, you are subject not only to dealing with the disease yourself, but also to be raised in a dysfunctional situation.

From **Sugar and Salt : My Life with Bipolar Disorder**

by Jane Thompson

THERAPY

Bipolar disorders include Bipolar I, Bipolar II Disorders and others. These simply mean that depression and manic or hypomanic states alternate with each other in an individual. Features associated with bipolar disorders are suicide, child abuse, spousal abuse or violent behavior which may occur during severe mania or those with psychotic features. Other features include school truancy or failure, workplace failure, divorce, eating disorders, attention-deficit/hyperactivity disorder, panic disorder, social phobia, and substance abuse."

From **Diagnostic and Statistical Manual of Mental Disorders.**
American Psychiatric Association (1994).

There are about five million adults with bipolar disorder in the United States. The disorder is a genetic one, so people with bipolar disorder are often raised in a dysfunctional situation, with verbal or physical or sexual abuse present, making it difficult to sort out the causes and implications of the illness. It also makes it difficult to recognize what is normal.

As a child, I was raised in a dysfunctional situation in which my father was bipolar. This makes the disorder and the mood changes and the situations that arise from it seem more normal to the person. This can make the person less able to recognize the disorder in him-or her-self.

In my family, we walked on eggshells around my father, never knowing what mood he would be in or what would be acceptable. It is a huge light bulb that goes off when the person realizes the situation, and begins to see the number of people who surrounded him or her are also suffering with bipolar disorder. This can make the person more willing to be diagnosed.

This can go far in explaining childhood abuse and situations, and make it easier to deal with in therapy. It is also the reason that many people with bipolar disorder need therapy--just taking medication may not be enough to lift them out of the morass they are in.

Jut as bipolar disorder has several types, therapy used to treat bipolar disorder can be of several different types. Some therapies implemented are behavioral therapy, cognitive therapy, dialectical behavioral therapy, eye movement desensitization reprocessing therapy, family and marital therapy, and group therapy.

- Behavioral Therapy: This type of therapy is aimed at altering behavior. Dr. Phil, for example, is a behaviorist.
- Cognitive Therapy: This therapy is aimed at how a person processes information. It works on errors in thought, self-defeating conclusions, incorrect interpretation of information, and lack of adequate problem-solving strategies.
- Dialectical Behavioral Therapy: This therapy maintains that some people, due to invalidating environments during childhood and biological factors, react abnormally to emotional stimulation.

- Eye Movement Desensitization Reprocessing Therapy: A therapy for post traumatic stress disorder. It treats anxiety, stress and trauma.
- Family/Marital Therapy: This therapy deals with communication and conflict within relationships.
- Group Therapy: This therapy is used to work with groups of people, allowing peers to aid each other in working out problems

Therapies are not effective until proper medication has been prescribed and put in place. Unless and until the person with bipolar disorder has had his or her moods stabilized through medication(s), he or she is able to make only limited use of therapy. When moods are out of control, the ability to listen, hear, and alter behavior is simply not present. Without medication, you are not able to monitor yourself and accurately report your changes.

This is not to say that participating in therapy while not medicated is useless. It can make the person feel better to vent and to talk about his or her problems, but real progress cannot be made without the help of medications which will keep mood from swinging.

The most common therapy for bipolar disorder is cognitive therapy. In this therapy, the therapist attempts to get the person to see that he or she is making false assumptions or interpreting information incorrectly, coming up with conclusions that do not match reality. Behavioral therapy is also commonly used, in which the person's behavior is altered to allow him or her to interact more comfortably with the world.

Group therapy is also common, in which members of a group discuss and offer feedback on a patient's assumptions or problems, allowing the person to see them from many different angles. A doctor or therapist generally leads a group.

Therapy is not necessarily essential for recovery from bipolar disorder, but it can help. The genetic basis for the illness can aid in doing away with blame for the illness and its effects, but some people still need help in dealing with the abuse and chaos they grew up in. Therapy can help in sorting this out. Therapy can help one understand what "normal" is.

At some point during this time I attempted suicide by taking a bottle of tranquilizers. Of course they didn't hurt me a bit, they just made me oversleep, but I hadn't realized they were harmless. When Bill found out about it, he just assumed it was an attention-getting device. I told my OB-GYN about it, and he said that he would never have given me anything that I could hurt myself with, because he knew I was depressed. He suggested therapy, but I was not willing to attempt it. I was afraid of therapy. I was afraid it would somehow fundamentally change who I was. I refused to try. It sobered me up some, because I didn't want to die, I only wanted to stop feeling so miserable. And, of course, within a few months I was feeling on top of the world again....

For the first time, I felt that I needed help with my problems. I couldn't afford a private therapist, so I went to Dallas County Mental Health, which charged on a sliding scale. They saw me on a weekly basis, and immediately diagnosed me as depressed. My sessions consisted of one-on-one counseling with the therapist explaining to me that I was an attractive, intelligent woman who had a lot to offer and that I shouldn't be depressed. "You should just get over this depression. It is serving no purpose for you. "I asked him over and over how I was to do that and he said that I should just not be depressed. "What you need to do is just start feeling better." After about four meetings, I couldn't take any more of this and stopped going to counseling.

This was actually quite a negative experience for me, for it convinced me that counseling and therapy offered nothing to me and it would be years before I would try again.

From **Sugar and Salt : My Life with Bipolar Disorder**
By Jane Thompson

DUAL DIAGNOSIS

It would be hard to find a person with bipolar disorder who didn't "self-medicate" with drugs. Often the drug-taking gets in the way of the diagnosis, as people assume that the behavior is caused by the drugs the person is taking. In my book, **Sugar and Salt,** I related an experience with an undiagnosed bipolar I was dating (I was undiagnosed at the time, too) who would wake up and either take a hit of speed or smoke a joint before he started his day. At the time, I was completely confused by his alternation between drugs; now I can see that he was trying to calm himself down or bring himself up by his choice of drug. Self medication does not work and always makes the situation worse.

During this time I discovered that I could sleep through most of the night if I smoked marijuana before I went to sleep and for ten years I did that. I only stopped when I was diagnosed and my doctor told me it would interfere with my medications. Since my medications allowed me to sleep, I was able to stop smoking marijuana immediately.

When trying to find peace or to stabilize one's feeling, people frequently self-medicate. The drug of choice for people with bipolar disorder is cocaine. Many people with bipolar disorder become involved with this drug and have to get off of it to be successfully medicated. Since cocaine can cause bizarre and unreliable behavior, it often delays the diagnosis, sometimes for years.

Another drug of choice is alcohol when self-medicating. Alcoholism and bipolar disorder go hand-in-hand and again can delay the diagnosis. The person is often addicted to alcohol, and must break that addiction to be medicated. My friend Natalie thought she was having a wonderful time drinking every night. She reports passing out nightly and sometimes waking to find that she had vomited in the night. She partied nightly and went through three evictions, her car being repossessed, and had two drunk driving convictions before she realized that alcohol was not her major problem. She has since been stabilized on medication and has her life back on track.

Besides these drugs, many people with mood disorders are smokers. It is almost impossible to quit smoking until stabilized, and most doctors do not recommend that you try. I smoked for thirty years and did not quit until I had been stabilized for fifteen. Nicotine seems to calm the bipolar mind.

You cannot mix illegal drugs with medications. The illegal drugs will destabilize you and work against the medications. All doctors and experts agree on this important point.. The only exception is a little wine occasionally, if you are not addicted to alcohol. I usually just tell people that I can't drink, that alcohol interacts with my medication. In order to be well, you have to be drug and alcohol-free.

After a couple of years, I began to notice a pattern and kept track of his visits. I usually saw him once, twice, or three times a week for about six weeks, and then for about three weeks I didn't hear from him at all. This pattern stayed true, but I couldn't figure out why. He changed jobs often.... He had other habits that completely confused me. Some mornings he would get up and take an upper. Some mornings he would swing his feet out of bed and smoke a joint. I could not predict which it would be and I never understood how he chose his drug.

It was years later that I realized that he, too, was manic-depressive and was doing what so many of us do--self medicating in an effort to make ourselves feel better. It was during my time with him that I started smoking marijuana to help me sleep.

From **Sugar and Salt : My Life with Bipolar Disorder**
by Jane Thompson

DEALING WITH DOCTORS

If you have bipolar disorder, of if you have a loved one with the disorder, don't give up looking for that balance and stability that is possible. You have the right to stability, to get off the roller coaster that controls you.

From **Sugar and Salt : My Life with Bipolar Disorder**
by Jane Thompson

You should be going to a psychiatrist, where you will be talking with him and perhaps a psychiatric nurse. The most important thing when dealing with professionals is to always be honest. There is not much--hardly anything--that you can say that they haven't heard before. I once counseled a woman who said she was too embarrassed to tell her doctor something; that she was spending her money so fast that she did not have rent money at the end of the month, then had to scramble every month to make the rent. I convinced her that overspending was a common symptom of bipolar disorder, that her doctor had surely heard that and worse before, and that he probably could help her with a medication adjustment. She agreed, then, that it was something she should share with him.

Most doctors do not do therapy. They concentrate on medications and finding the right combination that will work for you. If you want therapy, you will need to find a therapist separate from your doctor. He or she will need to know how you are reacting to your medications and what symptoms you still have with them. Side effects from your medications are important. When you are just being stabilized, it is a good idea to write everything down so you remember it for your appointment.

It is important that you can rely on your doctor and that he cares what happens to you. Even if you are stabilized and everything seems fine, you never know when an emergency could come up and you will need a doctor who will respond. Routine can go sideways fast.

Your doctor does not have to be your friend, but he or she should be someone you have trust and confidence in. One of my doctors, when I told him that the med I was taking was not working, told me that I was not the judge of that, he was. This is not acceptable. You are the one who decides if a medication is working, after giving it enough time to find out, of course.

A hint for dealing with doctors: They are people too, and one of the ways they judge your mental health is how you look. If you are feeling good and don't want any changes in your care, look as good as you can. If you are not feeling well, if you are depressed or are going into mania and you know you need a change, then deliberately go in looking not quite as well-groomed. They will pick up on this and perhaps be more willing to listen. Women, don't wear your makeup. Men, don't shave or perhaps wear unpressed clothes. Believe me, it works.

But, as I said, trust in your doctor is the most important thing. He needs to be on your team. You don't have to like him, but you need to feel that he knows what he is doing and that he has your best interests at heart. It does not mean that he will always do exactly what you want, but he should listen to you and at least consider your suggestions.

MEDICATION

The essential element in preventing episodes and staying stable is medication. You must take medication daily to prevent mood swings. That actually sounds pretty easy, but the process to find the right medications for you is one of trial and error and that takes some time. When I was diagnosed, there were not many medications that worked, and it took me five years to find the right medication. Now, there are many more to choose from and it generally does not take that long.

If you had heart disease, you would have just a few medications to choose from and they would work the same for everyone; but medications for the brain are individualized. What works great for your best friend may not work at all for you and may serve up awful side effects for you, too. You have to try a med, find that it does not work, then try another. You may have to try as many as four or five before you find the right combination. You usually do not take just one med, but a combination, often an antidepressant, a mood stabilizer, and an anti-psychotic. Along with those, or some other combination, you may also need something for sleep or for anxiety.

The purpose of these medications is to reach stability, a state in which you do not fly with mania or dip to the depths with depression. I have been stable for 20 years, so I know it can be done with patience and persistence. I think the most important factor in reaching stability is a person's attitude toward medications. Some people resent taking them, almost irrationally. They complain about having to take them every day. As a friend said to me, "People have to eat every day, too, but they don't complain about that."

Alternative treatments, consisting of vitamins, amino acids, and herbs, are touted on the Internet. These treatments do not work. In my opinion, they seem to work because some people have long periods between episodes. In these periods between episodes, alternative treatments appear to work; however, when an episode does occur, it leaves the patient without a safety net. He or she has no safety net just at the time when they need it the most. Prescription medications are the only things that have been clinically shown to stop the swings of bipolar disorder.

One of the biggest obstacles with psychiatric medications is their cost. Some of them are available in generic form, but most of them are so new that they are not. However, they can often be obtained free or at a low cost at a community Mental Health Clinic. Mental health treatment can be obtained even if you have little or no income if you are persistent and patient; however, one must ask for it.

The most important factor in dealing successfully with bipolar disorder is the person's attitude toward medications. The person who resents taking them will have much more difficulty than the person who sees them as a way to improve his or her life.

MEDICATIONS

Mood Stabilizers

Lithium
Depakote
Keppra
Lamictal
Neurontin
Tegretol
Abilify
Topomax
Trileptal

Antidepressants

Remoron
Cymbalta
Effexor
Wellbutrin
Celexa
Lexapro
Paxil
Prozac
Zoloft

Antipsychotics

Clozaril
Rispirdal
Zyprexia
Seroquel
Geodon

Anti-Anxiety

Klonopin
Valium
Xanax
Ativan
Dalmane

Google these medications to find out how they work and to discover any side effects.

...I was able to try Tegretol and within a week I was feeling better. I was stabilizing and soon felt better than I ever had. I was able to take things in stride and felt more in control of myself than I ever had. I felt like someone had given me the key to let me out of hell. No longer did I have to think about suicide all the time. My moods didn't plunge me into the depths or raise me to the heights. I felt "normal."

From **Sugar and Salt : My Life with Bipolar Disorder**
by Jane Thompson

RELATIONSHIPS

As a person with bipolar disorder, you probably have already had volatile relationships. This can apply to relationships with family members as well as love relationships. It is difficult to keep up with someone whose moods keep changing, and who can be irritable and angry for apparently no reason. We also tend to be obsessive with our relationships.

Another problem that I had and many others have is that it seems we are attracted to other people with bipolar disorder or other mood disorders. This can really make for exceptionally difficult relationships. When I was undiagnosed, I had one relationship with another undiagnosed bipolar that went on for ten years, with more difficulties than you can imagine. My ex-husband was bipolar, as were most of my boyfriends.

Even after I was diagnosed and stabilized, I still kept hooking up with guys with bipolar disorder. I would try to help them, but they didn't want to hear it from me. Inevitably, the relationship would founder.

I have never been involved in a relationship between two stable, medicated bipolar persons, but can imagine that would be a lot easier and much more successful than when only one person is stable. You could watch out for each other and help to monitor one another's moods.

If you are already in a relationship when you are diagnosed, the important thing to keeping that relationship healthy is to educate your partner. He or she is still with you, so that partner is already aware of some of the down side of being with a person with bipolar disorder. By knowing how the illness works, and what steps you will be taking as one reaches for stability and wellness, he or she can be great comfort and support.

Family members should also be educated about bipolar disorder. No one should have to go it alone; it is a rough ride and you need all the support you can get. In my case, my family denied the illness and I did have to go it alone in terms of family, but I did have friends who were willing to support me in my journey. Facing bipolar disorder, knowing it is a lifelong illness, is scary, and you should get as many people on your side as you can. Education as to what you are going through is key. As you educate yourself, take your support system along for the ride.

If you have already come to the point of diagnosis, then you know you have to change. One of the scariest parts is wondering how those you love will accept and go along with these changes in you. The best way to reach acceptance is to not be secretive about what you are going through, but to ask them for help. Be open and honest with them.

Now, when I say this, I don't mean that you should shout your diagnosis from the rooftops. There is a lot of stigma against mental illness and bipolar disorder in the world and in the workplace in particular. I'm talking about those lovers, relatives and close friends who make up your support system in your daily life and can help you on your road to stability. Those people who can help you to see your path, help you monitor your moods, and just listen when you feel like the world is caving in on you...these are the ones who need to educated about bipolar disorder. These are the people you trust and rely on.

I settled into being a housewife for the first time in my life and of course fell into a deep depression. I was miserable, felt I was in a deep hole that I couldn't get out of, and wanted to die. I had no friends, no function. I spent most of my time reading and did little else. Bill introduced me to one couple, but I had little in common with them. We fought. At one point he hauled off and hit me, hard, the only time he did that in our marriage. It scared me badly, because I lost the hearing in one ear.

From **Sugar and Salt : My Life with Bipolar Disorder**
by Jane Thompson

CREATIVITY

There has long been an acknowledged link between creativity and bipolar disorder. It doesn't mean that every person with bipolar disorder is blessed with great talent, but most of us do have a creative streak. It starts with Vincent Van Gogh, who was never formally diagnosed, but who was so frustrated at one point he cut off his own ear, and whose "Starry Night" could be titled "A Maniac's View of the Night Sky." It is another way of not feeling alone, seeing a list of famous people who have lived with manic depression. The list I offer here is only a partial one:

- Ludwig Von Beethoven
- Danny Bonaduce
- Art Buchwald
- Tim Burton
- Jim Carey
- Dick Cavett
- Winston Churchill
- Francis Ford Coppola
- Robert Downey Jr.
- Patty Duke
- Carrie Fischer
- Connie Francis
- Jimi Hendrix

- Edgar Allen Poe
- Axl Rose
- Theodore Roosevelt
- Robin Williams

You are probably not surprised to see Edgar Allen Poe or Jimi Hendrix on the list, but it may surprise you to see Winston Churchill. He was able to work unceasingly, to write voluminously, and to come up with many ideas. He, for example, came up with the idea for the tank. His associates, however, say that he had many ideas that he had to be talked out of, because they were so outlandish, and he writes himself of the "black dog" of depression that followed him all his life.

It makes me feel better about myself to know that people with bipolar disorder have been able to accomplish so much in the arts, and in such fields as politics. Patty Duke writes extensively of her bipolar disorder in her autobiography **Call Me Anna** and how it affected her life as an actress.

No one has ever suggested it, but it is my opinion that Judy Garland, with her phenomenal talent, problems with drugs and alcohol, extreme need for attention, and suicide attempts suffered with bipolar disorder. No one has ever suggested that, but she certainly showed all the signs. That is only my opinion, however, and is not by any means an official diagnosis.

While many of manic depression's victims have lived tempestuous lives that ended in suicide or confinement in mental institutions, they may also have made brilliant contributions to society: Lord Byron and Edgar Allen Poe, Anne Sexton and Virginia Woolf, Vincent Van Gogh, who completed more than three hundred paintings in the year and a half before he killed himself. Their names form an impressive honor roll of creativity and accomplishment.

From **A Brilliant Madness: Living with Manic Depressive Disorder**
By Patty Duke and Gloria Hochman

POOR JUDGMENT

One sign of mania is poor judgment. This can mean poor judgment in all areas of your life, your employment, your relationships, your spending, or, say, reckless or drunk driving. I have heard stories of people who started businesses they were not able to fund or successfully run, people who spent their rent money on frivolous things, people who hooked up with definitely the wrong people for them.

I used to pick up hitchhikers, just to have someone to talk to. Once I allowed a pair of hitchhikers to use my home while I was out of town for the weekend. This kind of thing is definitely poor judgment. When you start making these type of decisions on the job or in your business, it will destroy your life. When you spend your money on clothes and alcohol instead of on your house and/or your car payment, it will come home to roost rapidly.

Unfortunately, there is no law that exempts persons with bipolar disorder from paying bills incurred while manic. When the mania lifts, you are left with heavy debts that you often have no way to pay, or relationships that are fouled up, or results from trusting the wrong people. You have a hard time explaining it to yourself, much less to anyone else.

Some people make such bad decisions that they come into contact with the police and the justice system; again, there are no special rules for bipolar disorder. People who are manic cannot be talked out of their bad decisions, and will probably just have to pay for them later. The phenomenon of bad judgment is just another reason to stay on medication between episodes to prevent another from sneaking up on you and throwing you into another manic set of behaviors.

In 1987 and 1988, it was all I could do to pay for rent and food. I was barely making it and I was scared all the time. It was during this time that I can remember shoplifting. I stole some eye shadow that I wanted and couldn't afford from a grocery store where I was well known...I don't remember thinking about it or making a decision to steal it. It was there. I wanted it. I took it.

From **Sugar and Salt : My Life with Bipolar Disorder**
by Jane Thompson

SPENDING SPREES

Reckless spending is a common symptom of bipolar disorder. Many people see it as a failing and are ashamed of it. It can range from running up credit cards to making ridiculous purchases of thousands of dollars for things you don't remotely need. It goes along with mania and actually cannot be controlled by will power.

The only control for spending is medication and stability. I have heard of people spending thousands of dollars on cds, or going on ebay to buy things they have no need for at all. eBay or television infomercials can be real dangers to someone in the grip of mania. There are no special laws to get such a person off the hook for spending too much. Being bipolar or being manic is no excuse. Many people with bipolar disorder find that they have no recourse but to file bankruptcy, only to get themselves in financial trouble again.

Not being in control of our moods means not being in control of our actions. However, we are still responsible for them. This makes us responsible for obtaining treatment and striving for stability so we can follow the law. Being bipolar doesn't give us an excuse for spending, or for drunk driving, or any other actions we may perform while manic or depressed. Unfortunately, it is often these sorts of things that bring us to the breaking point of to finally being diagnosed.

It is usually our inability to conform our behavior that brings us in for diagnosis, no matter what it is. I was unable to work and was losing the ability to function normally when I turned myself in as a suspected crazy person. Usually it is a combination of things. I never have had the symptom of reckless spending, and my doctors cannot explain to me how I dodged that bullet. My father had that symptom, but my mother, who was not bipolar, was good at handling money. I seem to have gotten her knack for handling money while inheriting my father's bipolar disorder. I am grateful that I did not get that symptom, though I certainly manifested enough of the others. It is just an example of how individualized the disorder is, even though it is an easily described and recognized syndrome.

He [my father] had the emotional maturity of a two-year old. He had to have his way, and he insisted on being the center of attention at all times. He had no insight, and could not see that he had problems.... He resented his children because they took my mother's time and attention away from him, he let us know how unhappy that made him.... My mother would always calm the situation down. Her method was to protect him from reality as much as possible.... She handled the money because he could not be trusted to do so; she had taken over the money management when they were first married during the Great Depression and it became obvious that he could not restrain his spending.

From **Sugar and Salt : My Life with Bipolar Disorder**

by Jane Thompson

HYPERSEXUALITY

This is a symptom that no one really likes to talk about, but it is definitely there. It occurs with mania, not to everyone, but to enough people with bipolar disorder to be a real problem. Sometimes it results in only inappropriate flirtations, but it can also lead to affairs outside of marriage and even to the breakup of marriages.

It seems odd, but the person experiencing this seldom feels any guilt. It just seems like a normal thing to do. I had numerous affairs while married, and while I took steps to make certain my husband did not find out, I did not at all feel bad about what I was doing. I was able to easily justify it.

Some people fall so far "in love" that they leave their spouse and children only to discover when the mania abates that they have created a huge mess, and one that it is difficult to remedy. Hypersexuality among single people leads to "one night stands" and promiscuity, but seldom to the complications that occur with married people.

Since it is a symptom, it is one of those things that cannot be managed with will power. It all seems quite normal at the time. Later, when the person is stabilized on medication, he or she is quite often appalled at his or her own behavior, wondering how they could ever have behaved so.

Certainly it is difficult for the significant other or the spouse to understand, though some try. They know it is not the normal behavior of the person they love and they chalk it up to the effects of the illness. But it does play havoc with relationships and can cause their dissolution.

It could be that a person could be better armed to manage hypersexuality after they learn that it is a symptom and that they are subject to it, but I believe that most people just go with the flow and let their feelings take them away. Mania is irresistible. Mania is not controlled by will power, no matter how strong it is. It takes proper medication to get it under control.

Soon I was a full-fledged "bar slut," sleeping with every man who frequented the bar. There were so many I can't remember all their names. I'm certain the men thought little of me, but I was convinced I was looking for love. Looking back on it, I wonder that I had the nerve to keep showing my face there.

From **Sugar and Salt : My Life with Bipolar Disorder**
by Jane Thompson

SUICIDE

I know you have cried, I know you have felt desperate, I know that you feel like killing yourself to make the pain stop.

From **Sugar and Salt : My Life with Bipolar Disorder**
by Jane Thompson

Suicide occurs in nearly twenty percent of bipolar people. No one wants to talk about it. It is a scary subject and people are afraid to talk about it. But anyone with bipolar disorder should be aware of what a large problem it is and be prepared for suicidal thoughts. They come with the depression cycle of the bipolar disorder, and no one is immune.

It is useful to know that suicide is often the result of an impulse. The person does not really think about or plan it, but simply succumbs to an impulse that comes over him or her. A person with bipolar disorder should be aware of this and should be ready to deal with these impulses. The old saying that "suicide is a permanent solution to a temporary problem" is a true one. The depression a person is feeling is temporary, even though it doesn't feel temporary at the time-- it will lift.

I have often dealt with this monster, the worst occurrences after I developed an allergy to my medication after twelve years of stability. I plunged into depression, and felt that everything was hopeless.

Rationally, I knew that if medications had made me stable before, they could do it again, and I just needed to be patient while the doctor found the right medications. Clinging to that knowledge led me through this time, even though it was difficult.

What got me through other depressions was simply the knowledge that I had felt better in the past, and that I knew I could feel better in the future. Also, curiosity about what was going to happen in my life next.

Bipolar people I have known who have committed suicides have used various methods, including gunshot, overdose, running a car into a semi. They were all done on impulse, not after long planning and thought. That is why I say a person with bipolar should think about suicide in advance and be prepared for these impulses. If you are thinking about and planning a suicide, you have plenty of time to contact your doctor, your therapist, or a friend to ask for help. But if it comes as an impulse, you need to have thought out your defenses in advance to be ready to reject the impulse and know in your mind that you need help and how and where to get it rather than acting on it. You must know that others need you and that your death will serve no purpose except to end the suffering at that second; you have many happy times ahead if you accept them. Listen to your rational mind, which knows things will get better with the right help.

I do know that at that moment it seems to be the only solution, but your rational mind knows better. Be ready for that moment and be ready to reject it. You can think of many arguments in advance as to why it is not a good solution and be ready to counteract them.

Just know that you, too, will have these thoughts and arm yourself against them. Be prepared to reject such an impulse--- recognize it, spurn it.

During this time I became very clever about how to obtain and stockpile pills--tranquilizers, usually Valium. At home, I picked fights with Harry; then I would fly into the bathroom and swallow half a bottle of whatever pills I had--Valium or Librium or Librax or whatever I have been able to get my hands on. These weren't real suicide attempts because I never did them unless someone, usually Harry, was there to make me throw up. I think they were a classic cry for help. It was as though there were demons inside me making me do all these crazy things. And the only way I could get away from them was a long sleep.

The real attempts to end my life didn't come until later.

From **A Brilliant Madness: Living with Manic Depressive Disorder**
By Patty Duke and Gloria Hochman

EMPLOYMENT

I was scared to death. One day I was just lying in bed, doing nothing, when I suddenly felt that someone had hit me in the back with a sledge-hammer. I was in incredible pain. I went to the doctor, and he told me my pack pain was caused by pure stress. I had made the decision to take a teaching job with a small private school, but the pay was so little I had to depend on my retirement from the state to make ends meet. The pain went away once I started teaching, but it was a sign of the fear and depression.

From **<u>Sugar and Salt : My Life with Bipolar Disorder</u>**
by Jane Thompson

It is often difficult to work when you are bipolar, particularly if you are not stable. Stress, in the form of deadlines and getting along with others, can cause you to "lose it" and make you into a problem for the boss. However, I think it is better to continue working as long as it is possible for you to do so. If you take time off to go on disability, the time off is hard to explain to future interviewers, and you can get out of the habit of working.

When I was both undiagnosed and diagnosed, I swore I would work until retirement. It didn't work out quite that way, but I certainly tried. I was laid off and fired from several jobs, but I kept going back for more. I supported myself through the worst of it. I wanted to take care of myself and could not see myself sitting at home without the social interaction and the satisfaction that work brought me.

From my own experience, the most important advice I can give is to not disclose your illness to your employer. I had been working at a job for seven years, had been given awards for being "dependable, dedicated, and determined" and felt I was secure when I suddenly developed an allergy to the medication I had been on for twelve years and had to go off this medication immediately--cold turkey. I would essentially be without medications while my doctor searched for the right ones for me again.

Thinking my boss would be sympathetic, I told her I was bipolar and that I was off medications for a few weeks. She immediately began writing me up for every problem and eventually fired me. There is a huge stigma that goes along with being bipolar, and employers are afraid you will do something violent on the job. The last thing you want to do is label yourself.

However, I still believe that working gives you an identity, helps you with your social life, and gives you purpose, and I recommend that you continue working if it is at all possible. At the same time, I know the frustration that goes along with it, the fear of being fired, the actuality of being fired, and how difficult it is to drag oneself to work after a sleepless night.

Work brings satisfaction and a reason to get up in the morning. It is much easier to do after you are stabilized on medication, and you may find after that you can hold a job for years. I know many people with bipolar disorder who have done it. It depends on the severity of the disease, the ease with which you are stabilized, and pure luck of the draw on your job.

Having said that, I also know that some people cannot work under any circumstances. In that case, you will need to apply for disability.

I struggled all my adult life with working at a job when I had one, finding one when I didn't one, and keeping one..., but my illness often caused me to lose jobs or not be able to find one. Stress was always difficult for me...for example, the stress of two print deadlines a month...kept me upset much of the time. I also clashed with co-workers, but usually got along well with supervisors....I was often without work, and when I was sickest, couldn't find or hold even temporary jobs.

From **Sugar and Salt : My Life with Bipolar Disorder**
by Jane Thompson

DISABILITY

If you find yourself unable to work, you can apply for disability. I was forced to do so after I lost my job at age 55, followed by two more job losses in rapid succession. If you have a history of working and enough quarters of work to qualify, you may apply for Social Security Disability Insurance. You can apply in person at the Social Security Office, or online at their Website. I have known people who received their benefits at their first application, but I was denied the first time.

My doctor recommended that I hire an attorney. There are attorneys who specialize in this practice; they take your case and are only paid if you receive benefits. If you are approved, you are eligible for benefits back to the date of your application. Likewise, the attorney will take 25 percent of these back benefits when they are awarded. After my second denial, my attorney filed for a hearing, and worked to collect papers and records that would document my disability.

It took a total of 22 months from the time of my application for me to receive a hearing. We walked into the hearing only to learn that it had already been determined that I was disabled. The panel already had gone over my papers and made the determination before the hearing had started. The hearing was just a formality. So I was qualified.

A person who receives Disability is also eligible for Medicare 24 months after his or her application date. This means you will receive health insurance and help with your medications. The wait will vary according to how long it took you to become eligible. I only had to wait two months, since it took me 22 months to establish my eligibility.

There is also a plan under Social Security Disability in which you can work part time or prepare yourself to go back to work full time.

But if you do not have a work history or enough work quarters to qualify for Social Security Disability, you can apply for Supplemental Security Income. This does not give you as much income as Social Security Disability, but is a regular monthly check that comes with Medicaid, a state-run health insurance plan with help for medications.

You may find that you can work part time while on disability, but after you have been on it for a while and not working, it will be difficult to explain the time off to a prospective employer if you do become stabilized on medications that will allow you to go back to work. However, it is an alternative which allows a person the dignity of income if he or she is not able to work.

The experience of being fired from the best job I had ever had broke my spirit. That's when I realized I would have to apply for Social Security Disability. In the past I had believed that was giving up, and that you had to keep trying. But now I knew I had reached a point where trying wasn't gong to get me there any more, that I had to admit that I was finally too ill to work…. I put my home on the market…and applied for Social Security Disability.

From **Sugar and Salt : My Life with Bipolar Disorder**
by Jane Thompson

SCHEDULES

One of the most important things you can do to take care of yourself is to put yourself on a schedule. Now, if that sounds boring, it is. But it is also essential. You have to give up those manic late night parties and those depressed three a.m. pity parties. You simply must ensure you get regular sleep. This means going to bed at a decent hour and getting up at a decent hour in the morning. Well, you say, I can't get to sleep. For the first time in your life, your doctor will listen to you when you tell him or her that you can't sleep and will give you medication to help you sleep.

My doctors always said, "You will sleep when you are tired." Well, we know that isn't true. With mania or depression, you may stay up for days. I used to beg for sleep medications, then carefully cut them in two so they would last longer. It was my first psychiatrist who made sure that I slept, and all my psychiatrists since have made certain that I was able to sleep. Sleep is extremely important to stopping the cycling, as staying awake can throw you in mania, which will start the cycle all over again.

But this requires regular sleep. Anyway who is stable will tell you that they live by a schedule. Your meals must be scheduled, also. There is no special diet for bipolar disorder, just good, nutritious food. Stuffing yourself with fast food never helps. Anything that can start you cycling by being a little off should be avoided. At first it seems artificial, but after you are used to it and no longer cycling, you see the value in it and it becomes both automatic and very essential..

One thing that seems common to people with bipolar disorder is the tendency to sleep during the day and stay up all night. It just seems to be a natural pattern for us. This is not something you want to get into. If you get into this pattern, it leads to cycling. It also cuts you off from the world and its rhythms and your support system. It also makes work extremely difficult if you are working or are looking for work. Once you are stable, it is easier to stay out of this pattern. It is not a beneficial one. If you do stay up all night, then stay up the next day so you can sleep the next night.

A schedule seems to be an important factor to stopping the cycling. Along with medication, it enables you to live a "normal" life by keeping you in the same time zone with the rest of the world.

If you're like me, and you're affected by lack of sleep or changing time zones when you travel, try to pace yourself. Allow time for a nap or just don't schedule yourself too heavily until you've rested.

And if you need to eat on time the way I do, make sure you do it. You don't want to be around when I'm hungry and the meal is taking too long to arrive.

From **A Brilliant Madness: Living with Manic Depressive Disorder**
By Patty Duke and Gloria Hochman

MONITORING

Another thing you must learn to do to manage bipolar disorder is to monitor yourself. This takes time and experience, and, if you have a significant other, requires help from him or her. Monitoring means watching for those tell-tale signs that you are going into an episode or are cycling. And these are extremely personal -- no one knows the signs like you do. No one knows yourself like you do.

Irritability is a sign for me. Changes in eating, in sleeping patterns may be one for you. It may mean that you need to change your schedule; perhaps you have not been getting enough sleep or have otherwise deviated from your regular routine. Perhaps you need to call your doctor for a medication change. But you are the only one who really knows what is happening. Pay close attention to what is happening when you see change -- what is changing in your routine?

This is not something you can do right away. It takes experience and it takes failure to really learn what is happening with your mind and body to allow you to predict what is going to happen. This is one of the reasons people who have just been diagnosed are often encouraged to keep a mood chart. You can chart changes in your mood, noting other changes in your life that go along with those changes.

But it is difficult to do. When I am irritable, it is hard to realize while I am being so irritable, that it is a sign of mania. Usually I just go on being irritable. It takes years to develop the ability to catch your moods while they are happening, and it takes years of failure to do so. "Oh yeah, I was irritable all last week, and now I am acting manic." After a few of these, you will start monitoring yourself for the warning signs of mood changes that will allow you to take steps to keep yourself stable.

A significant other can help, but at the risk of being told to mind his or her own business the first few times he or she tries to warn you that you are acting as if you are becoming manic or depressed. Somehow, we don't like to be monitored by others. But after a while, we can learn to take these warnings as they are meant, in good spirit, and use them to help us manage the illness.

Monitoring ourselves is one of the hardest things to learn and is also one of the most important. After some time, it becomes automatic and allows you to stay on top of the disorder.

Try to live as though you have a disease like diabetes. You have to know what you are dealing with; you have to monitor yourself and keep up with any changes in your illness. Everybody has something to deal with, we just have bipolar disorder. Sometimes I don't sleep, sometimes I get a little manic, but I watch myself and try to keep myself on an even keel. Pay attention -- are you sleeping? Are you pacing? Are you spending? Do you lose your focus? Are your medications making you feel peaceful and stable? Or do you feel out of control and irritable? Are you blowing things out of proportion? Seek the peaceful, self-confident, and stable. Perhaps your medications need to be changed or it's time to change doctors. Nothing about bipolar disorder is easy. It's not easy living with the roller coaster ups and downs of the illness, the diagnosis is not easy, and it's not easy finding the right medications. You have to stay on your medications, monitor yourself, and stay under a doctor's care for the rest of your life.... It is a lifelong fight and you can never give up.

From **Sugar and Salt : My Life with Bipolar Disorder**

by Jane Thompson

HOSPITALIZATION

Hospitalization doesn't have to be as bad as it sounds. Of course, it all depends on whether you are hospitalized against your will. In that case, you generally are so upset that it takes you a while to calm down and get any benefits from the experience.

I was hospitalized once, and it was voluntary. I could not find the right medications, and I had tried for five years. Somehow it seemed that if I didn't do something different, I was just going to keep trying without making any progress forever. So I checked myself into a teaching hospital, and within a week I was placed on the correct med for me and my life changed.

At the same time, it was not a completely positive experience. The liability is so great if a patient commits suicide in a hospital (and it does happen) that there are all these tremendously picky rules that will drive you crazy. You just have to learn to live with them and laugh about them if you can.

One thing about the hospital is that you will meet interesting and nice people--I'm talking about the other patients. You can exchange stories and find out what other people are dealing with. That generally makes you feel better about your situation. I have known many people who have gone into the hospital on a voluntary basis to get their medications straightened out and they generally are glad that they have made the move.

However, if you have been committed to the hospital, it is a different story. You are usually frightened and resentful, and so focused on yourself and what is happening to you that you don't get much of the positive experience that a voluntary patient does. You just want out, and you are not very cooperative. Some people find that at the end, they have received help and gotten on medications that stabilize them, but most seem to be resentful that they were locked up against their will and do not have good memories or results from being committed. It seems to be the quality of the institution and how they treat patients as to what the outcome is. But no one likes to be forced to do anything.

If you find that you must be hospitalized for any reason, try to make it a positive experience. Try to learn as much as you can and try to work with the staff to reach good outcomes for yourself. It is certainly not a pleasant situation, but humor and friendship can be found anywhere, and, as in my case, it may be the move you need to make to get a handle on your illness.

When I saw the young residents and interns scurrying around the ward, I realized that I had done something I always had been advised not to do! I had checked myself into a teaching hospital at the end of June just before the new crop of interns and residents came on board. Before joining the population, I was briefed on the rules. (I was to learn how important rules/schedules/routine can be to the manic-depressive person.) Smoking was allowed on this ward only (because it is so difficult for people with mood disorders to quit smoking). I was supposed to take part in all activities, to keep my room neat, and to ask permission to do just about anything....

I would be undergoing testing for just about everything--and I would be cooperative.

From **Sugar and Salt : My Life with Bipolar Disorder**
by Jane Thompson

STIGMA

There is a great deal of stigma attached to mental illness, and especially to bipolar disorder. When you are first diagnosed, you may have a tendency to tell everyone about your diagnosis, if only to explain your former actions. This is not really a good idea and I would certainly advise against this impulse. You should, of course, tell your family and your closest friends. This, however, is when you find that some people who you thought were your close friends are not your friends at all. When I came home from the hospital, I told a friend, and she simply hung up the phone and never spoke to me again. It is a good way to find out who your true friends are.

It is a bad idea to let those you work with or for to know that you are bipolar if you can avoid it. Employers are afraid that if you are bipolar that you will do something violent in the workplace. They will do all they can to get you out of the workplace and worry about the consequences later. If you co-workers find out, you will find yourself the target of gossip and innuendo about your ability to do the work and your ability to get along with others.

You will need the support of your family and your friends if you are lucky enough to get it. Sometimes families are not as understanding as we would like, and sometimes we have to make new friends. It is a fact of life that the stigma against the illness exists and that we must live with it. I found that my family was not at all supportive; in fact, they completely denied my illness and I had no support there.

However, most of my friends were supportive and understanding so I found my support with friends. You can work to overcome the stigma by living your life in a rational, stable way so that when you have to announce your illness people can see that you are not some kind of scary monster. Also, try to educate people about bipolar disorder in a calm, rational way without giving away your status. There is a great deal of misinformation out there and you can address it whenever possible.

Fortunately, psychiatric conditions like bipolar disorder are not often considered "blemishes of individual character" anymore, but they are stigmatized just the same. Persons with psychiatric conditions are too often regarded as untreatable and thus unpredictable and dangerous, or at the very least unreliable and incompetent.

From **Bipolar Disorder: A Guide for Patients and Families**
by Francis Mark Mondimore, M.D.

BOOKS

So you have been diagnosed, and you are confused, or angry or upset, or relieved. What do you do now? If you are like most people, you want to learn as much as you can about the illness you have. When I was diagnosed, back in 1982, I went to the library, and by this time I was back in a big city, Dallas, and could only find one book on the subject. It was Dr. Ronald Fieve's **Moodswing**, which was a good book, but it left me with a lot of questions. (This book is now out of print, but can still be obtained on Amazon.com). He emphasized the symptom of spending sprees, which a lot of people in the manic mood undergo. But I had never had this symptom. Could it be that I wasn't manic-depressive, as it was called back then. Maybe I didn't meet the criteria for the diagnosis.

There was no Internet to go to and I had to wait until I could question a doctor to find out that spending sprees were a common symptom, but not a universal one. My doctors still can't explain to me why I don't have this particular symptom, even though so many others do. I felt so ignorant and I wanted information. Today there is a world of information at your fingertips. There are literally hundreds of books you can consult to learn about the disorder; I have listed a number of them. I have listed the "best" books about bipolar disorder in my opinion; it is in other people's opinions, too, including my doctor's. I have listed many memoirs. I think they are important for making you realize that you are not alone, that many of us suffer with this disorder and that many of our experiences are the same. How we came to our diagnoses, how we managed the illness, what our experiences were before we realized we were ill, those may differ, but it all comes down to one disorder and manias and depressions are essentially the same. With manias come poor judgment and sometimes psychotic symptoms; with depression; comes an inability to function. For me, I am unable to eat or sleep, whether manic or depressed. For a long period, I weighed only 100 pounds because I couldn't eat enough to keep the weight on. At least that problem is solved!

Of course, I listed my own memoir in that group of books, **Sugar and Salt: My Life with Bipolar Disorder**. When I wrote the book, I hoped I could reach people, make them see that they were not alone, and inspire them to reach out for stability and peace. I think that is the goal of most of those who write memoirs; they want to help others. It is also a kind of a therapy, to tell your story honestly and without holding back. Some people don't get it; I received some book reviews from people who thought that I was not describing bipolar disorder. I can only conclude that they were people without the disorder, who thought that they would see even more flagrant behavior from a mentally ill person. But my behavior was classic manic-depressive, keeping me from holding jobs and messing up my relationships. It was off-the-wall enough for me. I also received feedback from those who did get it; they could relate to my struggles and to the long road I traversed to stability and functioning.

BEST BOOKS
ON BIPOLAR DISORDER

I think the first book to start with is Patty Duke's **A Brilliant Madness: Living with Manic-Depressive Illness**. Patty Duke co-wrote it with Gloria Hochman, and in it they alternate chapters, with Patty describing the illness as it affected her, and Gloria describing the science. It is a good introductory book to the disorder. Patty has also written an autobiography about her illness, **Call Me Anna**.

Other excellent books are authored by Kay Redfield Jamison, herself a clinical psychiatrist who has bipolar disorder **An Unquiet Mind: A Memoir of Moods and Madness** is her memoir of her illness, describing bipolar disorder both as it affected her and from the perspective of a doctor. She began suffering mood swings as an adolescent, but did not seek help until after she graduated and began teaching. She experienced periodic depressions, which she thought she should work out herself, and her manias she saw as periods of creativity. Her book chronicles her realization that she needed help with her disease.

Ms. Jamison has also written **Touched with Fire: Manic-Depressive Illness and the Artistic Temperament**. In it she continues her autobiographical story as it refers to creativity and bipolar disorder. With great honesty she tells of the costs of the illness and the benefits that may come with it. She also argues that most artistic geniuses were bipolar.

She also wrote **Night Falls Fast: Understanding Suicide**. Since she suffers from bipolar disorder, she understands this first hand, having planned and attempted her own suicide. She identifies suicide as an often preventable medical and social problem and discloses interesting facts about suicide in her study.

GENERAL BOOKS ON BIPOLAR DISORDER

Other, more general books include **Take Charge of Bipolar Disorder: A 4-Step Plan for You and Your Loved Ones to Manage the Illness and Create Lasting Stability** by Julie Fast and John Preston. This book offers supplementary help besides medications, such as learning to identify triggers and helping you to manage your moods.

The Bipolar Survival Guide: What You and Your Family Need to Know by David J. Miklowitz. It covers the origins, symptoms, and treatments for bipolar disorder, with emphasis on current medications. It also contains information on resources.

Bipolar Disorder: A Guide for Patients and Families by Francis M. Mondimore, M.D. Dr. Mondimore discusses the diagnosis of bipolar disorder, the treatment, with special emphasis on side effects of medications, and how lifestyle changes can improve the quality of life. He also concentrates on how the disorder differently affects women, children, and adolescents. He also offers real, detailed help for living with the disease.

The Bipolar Workbook: Tools for Controlling Your Mood Swings by Monica Ramirez Basco. This book teaches readers to recognize and control their symptoms, cope, and to improve their self-esteem. It contains specific techniques, tools, and procedures that every patient can use.

Cognitive-Behavioral Therapy for Bipolar Disorder, concentrates on integrating pharmacological therapy with psychotherapy. Aimed toward the clinician, it can also be useful for the patient who is interested in how therapy and medication can work together to prevent relapse.

Living Well with Depression and Bipolar Disorder: What Your Doctor Doesn't Tell You…That You Need to Know by John Mcmanamy. This book is written by a patient, who discusses diagnoses, associated illnesses and symptoms, treatments, lifestyle, and coping, and the effects of depression and bipolar disorder on relationships and sex.

Bipolar Disorder for Dummies by Candida Fink and Joe Kraynak. This book reveals some of the causes and consequences of bipolar disorder, helps you with crisis survival strategies, and describes ways that friends and family members can support loved ones who have the disease.

The Bipolar Handbook: Real-Life Questions with Up-to-Date Answers by Wes Burgess. Dr. Wes Burgess answers 500 questions asked by his patients over the years. He covers every area of the disorder, from its causes to medical treatment and psychotherapy, and strategies for creating a healthy lifestyle.

New Hope for People with Bipolar Disorder: Your Friendly, Authoritative Guide to the Latest in Traditional and Complementary Solutions by Jan Fawcett, Bernard Golden, and Nancy Rosenfeld.

This book's primary focus is on the key issues in bipolar disorder: its genetic and biological basis; how psychosocial stress can alter its course; the problems of substance abuse; self-stigmatization and compliance; the impact of the illness on family, friends, and career, and treatment strategies.

The Bipolar Answer Book by Charles Atkins. This book, written by a psychiatrist, answers 275 questions about the illness. Questions include queries about symptoms, therapies, medications, and relapse-prevention strategies. It also covers what families and loved ones can do, what special issues there are for women, and how bipolar disorder differs in children and adults.

Bipolar Demystified: Mastering the Tightrope of Manic Depression by Lana R. Castle. Lana Castle is a woman who has bipolar disorder. She helps people to understand the true nature of the disorder, the factors that complicate its diagnosis, and strategies for coping with the illness.

Manic-Depressive Illness: Bipolar Disorders and Recurrent Depression (Second Edition) by Fredrick Goodwin and Kay Redfield Jamison. This is a scientific work, which surveys the massive body of evidence for a biomedical source or bipolar disorder. They review the biologic and genetic literature and incorporate research done since their first edition. Medical treatment is described, along with strategies to prevent future episodes given in detail, and special emphasis is given to fostering medication compliance and dealing with patients who abuse drugs and alcohol.

Surviving Manic Depression: A Manual on Bipolar Disorder for Patients, Families, and Providers by E. Fuller Torrey and Michael B. Knable. This book covers every aspect of living with bipolar disorder. Besides explaining what bipolar disorder feels like from the inside, the authors discuss causes and risk factors, medications and treatments, and ten special problems, including alcohol abuse and medical noncompliance.

Bipolar Disorder: A Cognitive Therapy Approach by Cory F. Newman, Robert L. Leahy, Aaron T. Beck, and Noreen Reilly-Harrington. This book discusses the interface between cognitive therapy and pharmacotherapy and offers ways for therapists to boost the morale, self-esteem, and hope and resiliency of patients through the therapeutic relationship.

Psychology Today: Taming Bipolar Disorder by Lori Oliwenstein. This book presents information, guidance and support people need in order to thrive. The book contains cutting-edge research and straightforward advice from the most respected names in the study of bipolar disorder.

Bipolar: Insights for Recovery by Jane Mountain who was an MD who gave up her practice to focus on recovery. She shares in everyday language the insights that have helped her and others on the path to recovery.

Crazy: A Father's Search Through America's Mental Health Madness by Pete Earley. Earley describes his attempts to get help for his bipolar son, while delving into the history of mental health treatment in this country.

MEMOIRS

Sugar and Salt: My Life with Bipolar Disorder by Jane Thompson. This is the story of an ordinary woman who was not diagnosed until she was 37. She undergoes a long fight to get proper treatment, goes back to work, then tragedy strikes as she is forced to change medications and loses her dream job.

Burn: A Bipolar Memoir by Shane Feldman. Shane was diagnosed as a child who was extremely intelligent but who had special needs. He was able to distinguish himself as a writer, and in 2001 he was diagnosed as bipolar.

Manic by Midnight by Faye Joy Shannon. This is the story of a woman with manic-depressive illness who was able to recover and live a happy and fulfilling life.

Living on the Edge of Madness by Sonny Kramer and Linda Wakeman. Linda Wakeman and Sonny Kramer had a relationship for twenty years; Linda suffers from bipolar disorder and Sonny writes her story.

In Small Doses: A Memoir about Accepting and Living with Bipolar Disorder by Marc Pollard. Frank prose describes the way Marc Pollard has written about his personal life with the disorder.

A Look Inside Bipolar Disorder--One Woman's Story by Suzanne Tracy Green. This book gives one woman's account of what her life is like on a day to day basis.

The Tattered Tapestry: A Family's Search for Peace with Bipolar Disorder by Tom Smith, Kevin Smith, and Karla Smith. The Smith family weaves threads of pain, confusion, grief, and hope into a moving portrait of the challenge and tragedy of bipolar disorder.

The Years of Silence are Past: My Father's Life with Bipolar Disorder by Stephen P. Hinshaw. Stephen Hinshaw describes life with a father who had great accomplishments, but periods of depression and institutionalization. It is a fascinating autobiography within a biography which seeks to explain the effects of bipolar disorder.

Edge of Sanity: Journal of Depression, Bipolar Disorder, and Beyond by Marlene Russell. This book speaks to people in everyday language about mental health disorders. Her intent is to promote openness and acceptance.

Detour: My Bipolar Road Trip in 4-D by Lizzie Simon. Her ingenious inquiry into the nature and treatment of manic-depression is spellbinding.

Electroboy: A Memoir of Mania by Andy Behrman. This is a blunt tale that relies on shock value to tell the story of the author's manias and his following depressions, as he bounces from fraud to jail.

Fevers of the Mind by Avery Conner. This story is about a young man who is diagnosed with bipolar disorder while performing research in neuroscience at Johns Hopkins University. He was able to continue his education and receive a Master's degree. He is optimistic about his illness and wishes to pass the optimism on.

Bipolar Disorder: A Family-Focused Treatment Approach by David Miklowitz and Michael Goldstein. This book presents the first treatment approach for bipolar disorder that truly integrates medication and family intervention.

Invisible Driving by Alistair McHaig. The manic narrator's voice vividly recreates the feelings and sensations of mania.

BOOKS FOR PARENTS
OF CHILDREN
WITH BIPOLAR DISORDER

The Bipolar Child: The Definitive and Reassuring Guide to Childhood's Most Misunderstood Disorder by Demitri Papolos and Janice Papolos. The material is presented clearly, with lots of helpful charts and lists to aid in receiving proper diagnosis, treatment, and long-term care.

Bipolar Disorders: A Guide to Helping Children and Adolescents by Mitzi Waltz. As many as a million children may have bipolar disorder in the United States. Families and communities pay a heavy toll when these disorders are not diagnosed and treated. Suicide, school failure, legal problems, limited job prospects, and hospitalization are possible outcomes. This book covers the topics that parents need to know.

The Ups and Downs of Raising a Bipolar Child: A Survival Guide for Parents by Judith Lederman and Candida Fink. For those caregivers who are looking for assistance and guidance from a parent's perspective, this book provides reasonable, commonsense suggestions that caregivers are likely to find quite helpful.

Survival Strategies for Parenting Children with Bipolar Disorder by George T. Lynn. George Lynn offers clear, practical advice on recognizing the symptoms, understanding medication, and accessing the necessary support at school as well as managing the day-to-day challenges.

New Hope for Children and Teens with Bipolar Disorder: Your Friendly, Authoritative Guide to the Traditional and Complementary Solutions by Boris Birmaher. In this book you will discover the compassionate and informative methods to help manage the diagnosis and help develop the natural strengths, gift, and skills that every child has to offer.

Intense Minds: Through the Eyes of Young People with Bipolar Disorder by Tracy Anglada. Young people and adults who grew up with the disorder speak out about how they experienced the disorder and how if affected their functioning.

Understanding the Mind of Your Bipolar Child: The Complete Guide to the Development, Treatment and Parenting of Children with Bipolar Disorder by Gregory T. Lombardo. The aim of this book is to provide a comprehensive overview of bipolar disorder in childhood, especial within the concept of development.

If Your Adolescent Has Depression or Bipolar Disorder: An Essential Resource for Parents by Dwight L. Evans and Linda Wasmer. This book is an authoritative guide that offers essential information such as how to go about getting a diagnosis, what the latest treatment options and strategies are, and how to help teens cope with mental illness at home and at school.

The Everything's Parent's Guide to Children with Bipolar Disorder: Professional, Reassuring Advice to Help You Understand and Cope by William Stillman and Jeffery Naser.

Bipolar Disorder in Childhood and Early Adolescence by Barbara Geller and Melissa B. DelBello. Geller and DelBello have done a great service to the field by pulling together into one compact volume the diversity of findings relevant to juvenile-onset bipolar disorder.

The Childhood Bipolar Disorder Answer Book by Tracy Anglada and Sheryl Hakala. The top 275 questions parents ask.

Connecting the Pieces: The Discovery of Early Onset Bipolar Disorder by Diane Kratt and Ethan Martinez. This story illustrates the importance of understanding mental illness as a brain disorder. It is actually a memoir of a mother and son's journey of understanding.

Mind Race: A Firsthand Account of One Teenager's Experience with Bipolar Disorder by Patrick E. Jamieson and Moira A. Rynn. A roadmap for young people living with bipolar disorder.

Brandon and the Bipolar Bear: A Story for Children with Bipolar Disorder by Tracy Anglada. This book helps to explain bipolar disorder and its treatment to children.

The Bipolar Bear Family: When a Parent Has Bipolar Disorder by Angela Ann Holloway. This book helps children address questions about bipolar disorder in a parent.

MAGAZINES

Psychology Today
Sussex Publishers, LLC
115 East 23rd Street, 9th Floor, New York, NY 10010

Bipolar Magazine
374 Delaware Avenue
Suite 302
Buffalo, NY 14202

Scientific **American Mind**
Scientific American Book Club
P.O. Box 6400
Camp Hill, PA 17012-6400

ALTERNATIVE TREATMENTS

If you are interested in reading about non-medical means of managing bipolar disorder:

The Natural Medicine Guide to Bipolar Disorder by Stephanie Mahron. This book profiles a range of effective, nondrug-based approaches that can restore health.

Healing Depression and Bipolar Disorder without Drugs: Inspiring Stories of Restoring Mental Health Through Natural Therapies by Gracelyn Guyol. This book discusses the underlying genetic, hormonal, and other underlying causes of depression and bipolar disorder.

SUPPORT GROUPS

One of the best ways to help yourself is to join a support group. I have listed places to find one in this book. These are informal groups that meet to talk with each other, to listen to speakers, and to work out problems that members may have. They may supplement or take the place of group therapy.

It is another way to not feel so alone, and to communicate with others who share the same problems and can help you to objectively solve yours. I made a mistake when I was first diagnosed. I had been going to a support group for only a short period of time when one of our member was involved in a shoot-out with police. She was a quiet, polite person and I liked her a great deal. I believe she was trying to commit "suicide by cop." The whole episode upset me a great deal and I never returned to that support group.

I believe I deprived myself of support and a chance to learn about others by dropping out of that group. I have since been very sorry that I quit going. I think I was scared by her actions and perhaps could not understand well enough what she was going through. Had I to do it over it again, I would return to the group and work through my feelings with the rest its members.

I think it would have done me good to understand her and to respond to the others' feelings. I could have worked through my own feelings and been much better able to deal with the confusion and feelings that were overwhelming me. Most groups are not faced with such a dramatic happening; most people are dealing with the problems of living with the disorder and have work and relationship problems. The whole group can tackle the problems and help the person get some perspective on what is happening. It is beneficial for all the members.

Sometimes an individual is depressed and can't see options clearly and the group can help with that, or the group can see warning signs that a member is starting to get manic. The feedback is invaluable in helping a person to learn to monitor himself or herself. One of the basic skills in taking care of yourself is learning to monitor your moods so you can tell your doctor how you feel and ask for adjustments in your medications.

When you are depressed, you often can't see ways you can help yourself, and a group can help you to get out of that box, help you to see that you need a med adjustment, and that there are things that you can do to help yourself feel better. The support of a group is invaluable.

SUPPORT GROUPS SITES

You can find support groups through:

National Alliance on Mental Illness
www.NAMI.org

Depression and Bipolar Support Alliance
www.Dbsalliance.org

Mental Health Centers in your community sponsor support groups

Many Hospitals, Catholic Charities and United Way also sponsor support groups

WEBSITES

You know you can get all kinds of information on the Internet. The problem is, where to find good information. You can Google literally hundreds of Websites on bipolar disorder. However, a good many of them are originated and maintained by pharmaceutical companies. They may, and probably do, give you good general information on bipolar disorder, but their reason for existing is to get you to use their medications. And it is not your job to decide which medication to use. You can make suggestions to your doctor, of course, but he is the expert and should be the one who decides which medications work best for you.

I have listed a few Websites that are helpful and from which you can start your quest for information. I start with government Websites because that is where you will get the most unbiased information. I go on to list organizational ones and even an individual one. You can Google as you wish. Just notice who owns the site and treat the information with that in mind.

You should probably not get all your information from one source, from books, or the Internet, or other persons with bipolar disorder. Try to balance it out; sometimes the person with bipolar can give you just the help you need right then, but other times a book will more thoroughly explain the complicated issues to you. The Internet is handy for quick answers and uncomplicated explanations. Use the resources in this book to find out all you can on bipolar disorder and how it will affect your life.

Knowledge is power. The more you know about the disorder, the more you can be ready for its effects and how to control them. You can learn to monitor the illness and know your triggers, but all this requires information about the disorder. Learn as much as you can; this will not only put you in control, but will also make you feel less helpless in the face of an illness that so many people feel controls them and that so many misunderstand or know so little about.

WEBSITE ADDRESSES

National Institute of Mental Health
www.NIMH.nih.gov
(with this one, it is easier to just Google NIMH)

www.nlm.nih.gov/medlineplus/

National Association Mental Illness
www.NAMI.org

www.nmha.org

www.WebMD.com

www.About.com

www.livingmanicdepressive.com

www.revolutionhealth.com

MESSAGE BOARDS

Message boards are one of the greatest and most accessible supports there are for persons with bipolar disorder. They offer instant help and support when you need help and advice, and just someone to talk to when you are lonely. They make you feel less alone, and if you are worried about a side effect from a medication you can get answers right away from others who take the same medication.

While every single case of bipolar disorder is different, you will find people who know what you are going through, how you feel, what you need in the way of support. I have made good friends from message boards.

You can remain anonymous and yet tell as much of your story as you want, and also offer support to others who are having difficulty. It is comforting to know that others know how you feel and have been through the same things you have. You can also talk, or at least leave messages, at any hour of the day or night. The people who post there certainly understand your situation and want to help you and may want help themselves. It is a nice reciprocity.

There is always a small group at any message board who comes there strictly for sympathy. They do not wish to take medications or, seemingly, to get any better. They just want sympathy for how bad they feel. Take the bad along with the good and try your best to remain positive. Most of the other people there are also trying to stay positive.

There are many message boards on the Web. I have listed just a few to get you started. Some of them I have used and found welcoming. I hope you can also receive help from them.

Some message boards have chatrooms associated with them. These allow you to talk with others in real time.

MESSAGE BOARD ADDRESSES

www.DrPhil.com

www.About.com

www.NAMI.org

www.bpbabble.com   CHATROOM

www.psychcentral.com   CHATROOM

THINGS I HAVE LEARNED

- *People are not pleased or intrigued when you get in touch with them after years of being out of communication. They probably remember you from a manic or depressed state and don't particularly want to go through it with you again.*

- *Don't continue with a doctor or dentist who seems to have a problem with your illness. Bipolar disorder will color your whole relationship with this healthcare provider, and he will not be able to treat or diagnose you properly.*

- *The doctor does not decide when your medication is right. You do. The proper medication fits you. It feels like a key slipping into a lock. On the other hand, no medication is perfect. You have to decide what side effects you can tolerate.*

- *Go to a psychiatrist. A medical doctor may have your best interests in mind, but he or she is not up on the latest mental health medications. They are coming out with new ones constantly. The ones I started on are not even being prescribed now.*

- *You always have options. There are community clinics everywhere. You may have to wait, but they have to see you. If you live in a state where mental health is not a priority, you may actually want to move to a place where more is spent on it. You may have to scrape up the money to go to a private doctor for diagnosis, and continue with a clinic when you find the proper medication.*

- *Mentally ill people are the most-discriminated against people in America today. Who else has special provisions in health insurance that only pays half of their care? You have to take care of yourself.*

- *Always make certain that every important interaction you have with a healthcare worker is properly documented. Use a tape recorder if you are worried. Your word is simply never taken. You are the crazy one.*

- *Be persistent. Especially with public mental health centers. You are just another person they have to care for. If you are not happy with your care, ask for a supervisor. You do not have to stay with the doctor you have been assigned to; you have the right to ask for another if you do not feel you are getting proper care.*

- *Bipolar disorder is not easily diagnosed. When it is diagnosed, it is not easy to find the proper medication. Lithium works for many, but not for all. It takes both patience and persistence. I was diagnosed in 1983 and did not find the right medication until 1988. Don't give up.*

- *Bipolar disorder is often confused with substance abuse. So many people with the disorder self-treat with illegal substances that it often confuses the matter. Are you taking illegal drugs to moderate your moods? Stop. It doesn't work and actually makes things worse.*

- *Never let your employer know you are bipolar. Most people are afraid of the disorder and have prejudices against those who have it. On the other hand, do tell your best friends and, of course, significant others. You need the support. I only lost one "friend" by telling her and, of course, decided she wasn't much of a friend. Those I told were otherwise unfailingly supportive.*

- *Explain it to people by telling them it is an illness like diabetes. Those with diabetes can't control their blood sugar and must take medication to control it; you can't control your moods and must take medication to help you control them.*

- *Regular sleep is all-important. Your doctor will help you to regulate your sleep; missing sleep may throw you into a manic state or deepen your depression. I take melatonin to help me go to sleep and sometimes I take generic non-prescription sleep aids. I have always had trouble going to sleep. Regularity in meals also will help regulate your moods. Get yourself on a schedule.*

- *Just because you don't have all the symptoms does not mean you are not bipolar. One of the more common symptoms and one that is always associated with bipolar disorder is spending sprees. I never really had that problem. I might buy a CD that I didn't really need or four lipsticks when I needed one, but I never spent myself into debt. Doesn't mean I wasn't bipolar. I just didn't have that particular symptom.*

- *People with bipolar disorder are often creative and sometimes avoid treatment because they fear it will stifle creativity. This is not true. I could never get it together to write before I had treatment because my thinking was too chaotic. If you read about individuals with bipolar disorder, many say they found their creativity more channeled and easier to manage after treatment.*

- *Join a support group if you feel the need. People there will understand your problems and offer help.*

- *Help your doctor understand your feelings by mirroring how you feel by how you look. Don't wear makeup and fix your hair if you feel rotten. (If you're a man, don't shave or press your clothes). Letting him or her see how you feel helps the doctor understand how you feel. Conversely, if you feel good, show it in the way you look.*

- *Do work with a doctor you feel comfortable with and you trust. While things may be going well now, you never know when an emergency is waiting around the corner. You don't want a doctor you don't feel comfortable with managing a crisis.*

- *One of the best pieces of advice I ever got was from a caseworker. If you feel yourself slipping into mania or depression, distract yourself. Don't sit around and obsess. Cook something, go for a walk, clean out the closet. It works.*

- *Being aggressive, raising your voice, or screaming and shouting, does not work*

- *Being assertive, asking for rights, demanding that you be listened to, does work.*

- *I take my nighttime medications a couple of hours before bedtime. That way the medications have time to start working before I actually go to bed, so I am ready for sleep when I do go to bed.*

- *When you are searching for that right combination of medications, keep a journal of your feelings and actions for the doctor. As your moods change, you may forget how you feel or what you did. When you go to your appointment, you will have something concrete to tell the doctor. This will help him/her know how you've been feeling and acting.*

- *If you feel alone, there are message boards for people with bipolar disorder. Dr. Phil, for example, has one. Here you can find support from people with the same problems as you have.*

From **Sugar and Salt : My Life with Bipolar Disorder**
by Jane Thompson

END WORD

If you have bipolar disorder, or if you have a loved one with the disorder, don't give up looking for that balance and stability that is possible. Don't let doctors tell you what works; listen to them, of course, try what they suggest and work with them, but when they tell you something works and it doesn't, move on to another doctor or another institution. You have the right to feel better. You have the right to stability, to get off that roller coaster that controls you. But, only you can do it. Nobody else can do it for you. Nurses, doctors, therapists can help, but they can't give you the motivation to keep working, to keep trying, to keep demanding the care you need to find that key that will let you out of hell. It's there, you just have to keep striving and reaching for it.

I know you have cried, I know you have felt desperate, I know that you feel like killing yourself to make the pain stop. But it doesn't have to be like that. You can smile, you can feel peaceful, you can feel like living. Believe me, it is all possible. If you know it is possible, you can work towards it with the knowledge that there is light at the end of the dark tunnel you are in. I've been in that tunnel and I know how you feel. When I was reaching for the peace of stability, I wasn't even sure I could reach it. I just knew I couldn't continue the way I was, and I didn't want to die. Doctors and nurses encouraged me to keep trying and my will to live made me believe that there was something better for me.

I was able to work for years without people knowing that I had a mental illness after I found the right medication. It was only the allergy that I developed to Tegretol that outed me. Employers and others have a great fear that persons with bipolar disorder will go postal at any time. We all must work to eradicate this stigma. People with bipolar disorder are much more likely to commit suicide than they are to hurt others. Suicide is a real danger for those with the illness; it is when we lose hope that things will ever improve in our life that we give up. Don't ever give up. Keep trying. There is always something more to try; another medication, another therapy. My life completely turned around. I've seen others' lives turned around by the right medications and the right therapies. You don't have to be left out. There are community mental health centers if you cannot afford private mental health care. Go to the hospital, like I did, if you need to. Make them listen to you. Don't be aggressive, but be assertive. It is worth it. You are worth it.

People with bipolar disorder often have to try many different medications to find the right one or the right combination. There is no one medication that works for everyone; just as everyone manifests the disease in different ways, everyone's body chemistry is a little different, and, unfortunately, the only way to find the right medication is by trial and error. This can be extremely frustrating but think of it as adventures in pharmacology. You are Alice in Wonderland wondering, "Hey, I wonder what this one will do?" And keep trying. You will find that key to let you out of hell. And that is worth it.

While people with depression will find their depression lifting after a time even if they do nothing, bipolar disorder cannot be controlled except with medication, and it is a lifelong commitment to take medication. As soon as the depression lifts, we are thrown into mania, which is perhaps not as unpleasant, but can have unpleasant consequences. Then, back to depression. It makes sense that groups like Scientologists, cults, do not want their members to take medications for psychiatric illnesses, for they often depend on brainwashing to keep their members compliant. And brainwashing is simply an induced depression.

Try to live as though you have a disease like diabetes. You have to know what you are dealing with; you have to monitor yourself and keep up with any changes in your illness. Everybody has something to deal with, we just got bipolar disorder. Sometimes I don't sleep, sometimes I get a little manic, but I watch myself and try to keep myself on an even keel. Pay attention -- are you sleeping? Are you pacing? Do you lose your focus? Are your medications making you feel peaceful and stable? Or do you feel out of control and irritable? Are you blowing things out of proportion? Seek the peaceful, self-confident, and stable. Perhaps your medications need to be changed or its time to change doctors.

Nothing about bipolar disorder is easy. It's not easy living with the roller coaster ups and downs of the illness, the diagnosis is not easy, and it's not easy finding the right medication. You have to stay on your medication, monitor yourself, and stay under a doctor's care for the rest of your life. Some people seem to feel that if they could just find that magic bullet, everything would come together and they wouldn't have to fight for their stability. But, there is no amino acid therapy, no nutritional therapy, no magic. It is a lifelong fight and you can never give up.

I have heard so many with bipolar disorder say that they "don't want to be on pills for the rest of their lives." I can't figure that one out. I would so much rather take a couple of pills a day than deal with mood swings, depression, irritability, inability to get along with others, mania, desperation, and all the other symptoms of bipolar disorder. And that part is easy. You just take a pill. Any fool can do that. Once you've found the right pill or the right combination of drugs.

Count on your friends, count on your family, and if you don't have their support, make your own by joining support groups and message boards. Learn as much as you can about the illness by researching it at the library or on the Web. But mostly, count on yourself. You can do it. I know it sometimes seems impossible, but the key is within your grasp. You just have to reach for it.

From **Sugar and Salt : My Life with Bipolar Disorder**
by Jane Thompson

Photo Credit: Ralf Kittenbacher, Alpha Photography

ABOUT THE AUTHOR:

Jane Thompson is a person with a breadth of experience. She has worked as a social worker, a teacher, as a paralegal, and, of course, as a writer. For years she wrote for the publisher of a political encyclopedia and served as a medical writer for a training corporation. **The Rookie's Guide to Bipolar Disorder** is her second book.